P9-CDB-875

The

BOY'S BODY BOOK

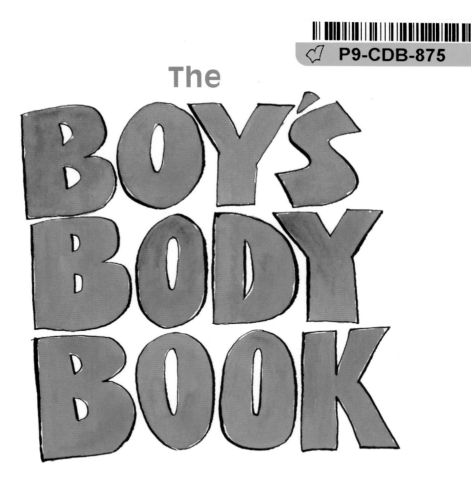

By Kelli Dunham, R.N.
Illustrated by Steve Bjorkman

Applesauce Press is an imprint of
Cider Mill Press Book Publishers

The Boy's Body Book

Copyright 2007, 2013, and 2015 by Appleseed Press Book Publishers

This is an officially licensed edition by Cider Mill Press Book Publishers LLC

All rights reserved under the Pan-American and International Copyright Conventions.

No part of this book may be reproduced in whole or in part, scanned, photocopied, recorded, distributed in any printed or electronic form, or reproduced in any manner whatsoever, or by any information storage and retrieval system now known or hereafter invented, without express written permission of the publisher, except in the case of brief quotations embodied in critical articles and reviews.

The scanning, uploading, and distribution of this book via the Internet or via any other means without permission of the publisher is illegal and punishable by law. Please support authors' rights, and do not participate in or encourage piracy of copyrighted materials.

13-Digit ISBN: 9781604335743
10-Digit ISBN: 1604335742

This book may be ordered by mail from the publisher. Please include $4.95 for postage and handling. Please support your local bookseller first!

Books published by Cider Mill Press Book Publishers are available at special discounts for bulk purchases in the United States by corporations, institutions, and other organizations. For more information, please contact the publisher.

Cider Mill Press Book Publishers
"Where good books are ready for press"
12 Spring Street
PO Box 454
Kennebunkport, Maine 04046

Visit us on the Web!
www.cidermillpress.com

Design: Alicia Freile, Tango Media
Typeset by Candice Fitzgibbons, Tango Media
Typography: Antique Olive, Berthold Akzidenz Grotesk, Bolten, Century Schoolbook, Frutiger, Gill Sans, Glypha, Imperfect, Monotype Sorts, Sue Ellen Francisco

Printed in China

1 2 3 4 5 6 7 8 9 0
Third Edition

Special thanks and acknowledgment to Josalyn Moran, an inspiration to every children's book publisher... and especially to us!

Dedicated to Heather Ann MacAllister, who every day makes the world a happier and safer place to be a growing boy.
-K.D.

TABLE OF CONTENTS

For Parents' and Teachers' Eyes Only!

Dear Parents and Educators:

As adolescents transition from childhood into their formative pre-teen years, they're going to have a lot of questions that they may be too afraid (or embarrassed) to ask you. More importantly, though, they will need to be armed with vital information that they may not be able to anticipate, let alone know how to ask for. Instead of turning to a friend or to the Internet for advice that may be questionable at best, pre-teens should be turning to *The Boy's Body Book*.

As an educator and school administrator with over thirty years of experience with both elementary and high school students, I know how essential it is for pre-teens to have resources readily available to them when they need to know about topics such as puberty, bullying, wellness, peer pressure, and even hygiene. The content, written by an R.N., is authoritative without being inaccessible to adolescent readers; this book will serve as the perfect conversation starter for you and your child or student—but you'll also find that pre-teens will delve eagerly into this book without your prompting. Feel confident when handing this essential guide to any adolescent that they will find this wealth of information both essential and empowering.

Wayne Woolridge
Superintendent of Schools (SAU29)

WHAT'S CHANGING?

AT THIS TIME in your life, on some days it might seem like… everything!

Your **body** is changing.

Your **feelings** are changing.

Your **relationships** with your friends and family members are changing.

It hardly seems fair, does it?

Especially because often as a boy gets older, he finds that it gets more difficult to talk with the adults in his life about the kind of things he used to. There are a few very good reasons for this:

He might be afraid to ask a question he thinks he should already know the answer to.

He might feel like he doesn't know the best (or the most polite) word to use to describe something that is happening with his body.

He might be worried that something he is feeling isn't normal, and that people would laugh at him if they knew what was going on in his head (or his body!).

Not very fun, but it is 100% normal!

Books = Food for your Brain

And it isn't just kids who sometimes develop troubles communicating. You may have noticed that sometimes the adults around you have trouble talking about the changes you are going through.

It seems like they should be able to handle it, since they've been through this hard "kid to adult" transition themselves. So what are they worried about? Mostly the same things you are!

There's no such thing as a stupid question.

They might worry about not having all the right information.

They might remember how awkward this time was for them and feel like they don't have any advice to help you get through it.

They might even be worried (does this sound familiar?) of not knowing the correct or polite terms for body parts and body processes.

And especially, they might be worried about giving you more information than you want to know or are ready for.

So with boys and adults all red-faced and stammering and stuttering it makes it hard for information to flow back and forth. That's where this book comes in.

This book has a lot of information about the changes that are coming your

way. We hope it will answer many of your questions so that you feel more ready and informed and less confused and scared.

Since this is an introduction, we'll take a few minutes here to introduce the topics to come. First up is a Chapter about puberty covering everything from growth spurts to body hair. In chapter 2, we'll talk about how to take care of your body now that it is getting all grown up. (Hint: Deodorant is your friend.) Chapter 3 goes into more detail about how to take care of yourself, including eating right, working your muscles, and getting enough sleep.

We're moving on to your social life in Chapter 4, talking about grades, study skills, and after-school jobs. Chapter 5 is about the changes you might see at home, such as curfews and changing family relationships. If you want to hear more about friendship skills or how to relate to girls, turn to Chapter 6, where we discover how your feelings and friends might be changing. Chapter 7 is very important. That's where we talk about keeping yourself safe both

on the internet and in the real world. Finally, Chapter 8 is all about common stressful situations, including divorce, moving, and out-of-control feelings.

Oh, almost forgot, at the very end, you'll discover some great resources that will be able to go into more depth about topics than we have room for here. Be sure to check them out if we haven't answered all your questions or you need more information.

There is no right or wrong way to use this book. You are the expert on how to make it work best for you!

You might want to sit right down and read it from cover to cover all at once (maybe under the covers with a flashlight, if you are feeling particularly shy).

You might just look at the chapters that interest you for now, and then put it on your shelf until you have more questions about the other stuff in the rest of the book.

If you aren't interested or don't want to know about the stuff in this book, no problem. You can always put the book away until later when you want to know more!

This is just one small book so it can't contain the answers for every question that you might have about this exciting—but sometimes confusing—time of your life.

QUICK TIP

If you don't like to read, (there are probably lots of guys who wish someone would develop an "all about your changing body" video game) you can ask an adult you trust to read through this book with you. Maybe you can use it as a starting point for a discussion about any questions you have.

Again, a trusted adult comes in handy. If something written here doesn't make sense to you, or is different from your experience, discuss it with a parent, teacher, health care provider, or another responsible, trusted grown-up.

Although this time is not easy, you already have many resources for dealing with the changes that are coming your way. You have past experiences that you have learned from. You have friends that are going through the same things you are, and you have adults who care about you. All these things will help make the process smoother. Best of luck to you as you begin the important transition of growing from a boy into a man.

I can do this!

I FOUND IT KIND OF EMBARRASSING TO TALK TO PEOPLE ABOUT MY BODY SO I WAS GLAD THERE WAS A BOOK LIKE THIS ONE. I USED TO KEEP MINE HIDDEN IN MY SOCK DRAWER WHERE NO ONE WOULD LOOK FOR IT.

Danny, age 15

Chapter 1:

YOUR CHANGING BODY (WHAT ON EARTH IS GOING ON AROUND HERE?)

If you are a boy between the ages of 8 and 12, you have probably noticed some changes in your body. These changes are called puberty. Puberty is the general name for the process everyone goes through to change from a kid to an adult. Some of the changes are physical and some of the changes are emotional.

Puberty takes place over several years, and while it may seem like the process will never end, most boys are through puberty by age 16 or 17 or so.

All About Puberty

The changes your body will go through can seem a bit mysterious, but they basically result from one thing: extra amounts of special chemicals (called hormones) that start to be produced in your body. In boys, the hormone most responsible for puberty is called testosterone. You'll be hearing a lot more about testosterone in the pages ahead.

Growth Spurts

One of the first changes you might notice is that you are growing quickly. During this rapid growth spurt, some boys find that clothes that fit at the beginning of the school year are too small by Halloween! Soon your shoulders will start to get wider and your muscles will start to develop more. You are on your way to achieving your adult body.

Hormones are chemical messengers that help your cells communicate with each other. Everyone has hormones. In boys the hormone that controls puberty is called testosterone. In girls, it's called estrogen.

Changing Body Shape and Size

One kind of annoying (and possibly embarrassing) part of the rapid increase in size and height is that your arms, legs, hands, and feet may grow faster than the rest of your body. So while the rest of your body is catching up, you might feel a little (or more than a little) clumsy. Sooner or later your body will once again be all the same size and you'll be back to your smooth self again.

Genital Changes: There's Something Going On Down There

One of the first changes many boys notice when they start puberty is that their testicles (the glands that produce sperm and testosterone) start to get bigger, and the skin on their scrotum (the pouch of skin behind the penis that holds the testicles) gets darker. If this is happening to you, you may also have noticed that the skin on your scrotum is starting to look rougher too.

Another thing you may discover is that because you have more testosterone in your system, you may have more frequent erections. Males are able to have erections (when the penis gets hard and sticks out more) even as babies; this is normal. But when these erections start happening more often (especially for what seems like no reason at all!) it can feel pretty embarrassing. Most of the time, if you don't make a big deal out of it, no one will

The male reproductive system is a pretty amazing bit of plumbing. It consists of the penis, the scrotum, the testicles, and the urethra. As you go through puberty you'll notice that you grow pubic hair (hair around and above your penis) and that your penis gets larger.

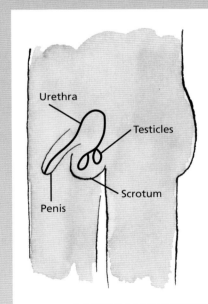

Urethra

Testicles

Penis

Scrotum

QUICK TIP

Some boys get embarrassed when they have a wet dream because the semen can make a mark on the sheets. If you feel this way, you might want to negotiate with your parents to do your own laundry. Then you'll be happy because you will be the only one who knows when you have a wet dream. Your parents will also be happy since it means they will have less laundry to do!

even notice you are having an erection. Especially if you are around other kids your age, chances are they are too busy feeling self-conscious about their own bodies to notice what is going on with yours!

Morning Surprises

Another thing that can sometimes embarrass boys going through puberty is something doctors call a "nocturnal emission" and everyone else calls a "wet dream." A wet dream is when some semen (the sticky liquid that is stored in the testicles) comes out from a boy's penis while he is asleep. Sometimes when this happens a boy remembers a certain type of dream; other times he just notices a wet spot on his pajamas or on the sheets after he wakes up.

If you don't know about this in advance, a wet dream can seem weird or even a little scary. But wet dreams are a normal part of development. They will stop happening as you get older.

The Expert Says

Everyone is concerned about what other people think of them, how their bodies look, and how they compare to others.

Body Hair

A big part of puberty is growing hair in all sorts of places you never had hair before!

Often the first place a boy notices hair growing is above his penis. Usually, the next place he becomes a little furry is the underarms, followed by the face, usually on the upper lip. When this happens, the exciting process of learning to shave is right around the corner. You can read more about shaving in Chapter 2.

WHAT'S THAT CRACKING SOUND: VOCAL CHANGES

When you are between 12 and 14 years old, your voice will start to get deeper. The deepening of your voice happens because of (bet you guessed this by now) the effect of testosterone. This time the testosterone is working on your larynx (also known as your voice box). The larynx then gets bigger and your vocal cords get longer and thicker.

For some boys, the voice change happens almost all at once; it seems like they go to bed one night with the voice of a boy and wake up the next morning with the voice of a man. Other guys may have months where their voice is higher at one moment and then lower a moment later. Sometimes a very quick change in pitch comes out as cracking. This might happen at very inconvenient moments: when you ask a question in class or when you are just about to get to the punch line of a joke. Fortunately, voice changes seldom take longer than 3-4 months to work themselves out.

KNOW THE FACTS

A boy's vocal chords grow 60% longer during puberty and become thicker. They go from vibrating 200 times a second to 120 times a second.

Finally, body hair begins to spread over the legs and arms. This can continue even a few years after all the other big changes of puberty have already happened. Some boys develop chest hair long after puberty, even into their 20s. But not all adult men have chest hair.

What's That Smell? Changes In Your Skin

You may have noticed (or someone might have told you!) that you are starting to smell, and not like a flower! As you go through puberty, the sweat and sebaceous (oil) glands in your skin become more active. This makes you sweat more. Because of hormonal changes, your sweat also has a different (some people say stronger) smell.

Your sebaceous glands are also pumping out more oil and this is part of what causes acne (also called "pimples" or the slang name "zits") in boys going through puberty. Acne and smelliness are normal, but there are ways you can take care of your skin to help decrease problems with both. You can read more about this in Chapter 2.

The Expert Says

Sweating is a healthy part of being active, so don't be embarrassed if you smell a bit after an intense game of basketball. Just take a shower as soon as you can.

Emotional Changes

Have you ever gotten to the point where you are happy one moment, furious the next, and then sad half an hour later? Welcome to one of the hardest parts of puberty: mood swings.

There are at least two reasons for mood swings. The first is the hormonal changes that are going on in your body. Yes, that pesky testosterone strikes again! The second has to do with your changing place in the world. Puberty is the bridge between being a boy and being a man, and sometimes you might feel like you don't belong either place. You aren't a kid anymore, but sometimes you feel like one inside and still want to do kid things. On

the other hand, you aren't ready for the responsibilities of an adult, even though you may feel like you want and need more independence. Some days you might feel out of place and like no one understands what you're going through. No wonder you might be a little (or a lot) cranky!

Talking about your feelings might help keep those emotions in check. Don't worry if it is hard for you to open up. Everyone feels this way sometimes. A trusted adult will understand if it is difficult for you to get the words out.

Hey, Am I Getting... Breasts?

Actually, boys do have breast tissue under their nipples. About half of all boys develop some swelling under their nipples as a part of middle puberty. The medical name for this is gynecomastia and it is a normal reaction to hormonal changes in the body. There are no medications that can make this swelling disappear; it just goes away on its own, usually in about six months. If you feel particularly worried about it, talk to your parents or a health care provider.

BOYS SAY:

FOR A WHILE I THOUGHT MY CHEST LOOKED WEIRD, LIKE I HAD LITTLE BREASTS GROWING THERE. IT WAS MOSTLY A PROBLEM IN THE SUMMER TIME WHEN EVERYONE WAS WEARING BATHING SUITS. I ASKED MY MOM TO GET ME A RASH GUARD SWIM TOP AND THAT REALLY HELPED. PLUS I DIDN'T HAVE TO WEAR AS MUCH SUNSCREEN.

-Robbie, age 18

REVIEWING:
WHAT'S NORMAL

◉ First of all, it's normal to feel unsure about the changes in your body. That's why this book was written, to help you sort out some of the questions you might have.

◉ It's also normal to develop more slowly or quickly than your friends and other boys you know. Every boy has his own pace for physical and emotional development.

◉ It's normal to feel unsettled about yourself and your relationships. Puberty is a very confusing and sometimes awkward time... for everyone. Right now feeling weird is perfectly normal!

◉ It's normal to have embarrassing things—like your voice cracking during a presentation—happen to you. At the time, it may seem like the worst thing that's ever happened in your life, but in a few weeks or a few months you'll forget all about it.

◉ It's normal to want to make changes in your life. You're growing up and things aren't supposed to stay the same.

◉ Asking your dad or mom or another adult to help you with whatever challenges you are facing as move through puberty is not just normal, it's ideal. That what your parents are there for!

◉ Growing hair in some unexpected places is totally normal. And if you don't grow hair in some places you might expect to, that's probably normal too. The hair might start growing in later, or it may not come at all.

◉ Looking to take on more responsibility, to be more in control of your life (even as your life seems to be more out of control) is normal. This is the time in your life when you are starting to gain a little bit of real independence. Your behavior will determine just how much impendence you can handle at this time in your life.

◉ So don't sweat it. It may take a little while, but sooner or later, you'll find that all these changes have sorted themselves out and you feel…perfectly normal!

QUICK TIP

Keeping a journal can help you feel more in control of your emotions. Getting those feelings out of your head and down on paper might help you understand a bit better why you are feeling like you do. You don't have to let anyone read (or even know about) the journal. It can be your secret. You can keep a journal on your computer or get a special notebook to put your thoughts in.

Chapter 2:

THE CARE AND FEEDING OF YOUR CHANGING BODY

It seems like it could be nature's joke that just when boys' sweat glands begin to work overtime, boys often develop what looks like an allergy to bathing. If you are struggling with the adults in your life about taking a bath (which does cut into video game playing time), remember this: Now that you are growing up, you have more adult-like sweat glands. This means you are going to have more of an adult-like smell. Even though you may not be able to tell the difference, people around you will. Especially at school, if you get the reputation as the "stinky kid," it could be very hard to lose.

Hit the Showers

Showering (or taking a bath) every day (or at least every other day) is your first line of defense when it comes to the "smellies." For best results, wash all your parts (from your head to your feet). Remember to use soap. Soap is an important part of this process and sometimes boys forget. If you have noticed that you are particularly smelly, you can get special soap labeled "deodorant," which will help keep you odor-free longer. It's best not to use deodorant soap all over your body though, because it can really dry out your skin. Just use it for your smelliest parts (usually your armpits and your feet).

Wash Those Hands

Hand washing is another important personal hygiene issue to talk about, and the good thing is that you don't even have to get completely wet to do it! Hand washing is not just about personal hygiene, because germs on your hands (which you use to touch everything) can make you (and people around you) sick. Sometimes it seems to boys that grown-ups are too worried about hand washing, but it is pretty important. If you eat without washing your hands, it's like (and yes, this is gross) putting everything

QUICK TIP

Taking a shower before you go to bed at night will help you get out the door faster in the morning. However, if you are particularly worried about the smellies, or you and your brother like to wrestle at night after you take your shower, a morning bath or shower is probably the way to go.

Lotion:
It's Not Just For Girls

You, yes you, can use lotion. Some boys will need lotion after a shower to keep from having dry, flaky, itchy skin. You can get lotion made especially for boys, and you can also get lotion that doesn't have any smell added to it at all. If you put in on while you are still damp from the shower, it will be a smoother process. You might even find that you like how it feels.

that you've touched since the last time you washed your hands… right in your mouth.

Not a very nice thought, is it? Yuck!

It's also very important to wash your hands after you use the toilet, after petting or handling any kind of animal, and if you have been around someone who is sick.

You already know how to wash your hands, right? Well, maybe so, but most people don't wash their hands long enough. It really takes 15 to 20 seconds under warm water (with soap) to get them clean. You might want to use a timer (or just count slowly to yourself) to make sure you're washing long enough. Sometimes dirt can get trapped under your nails: there are soft bristled brushes that can help with that.

Get Dressed

Showering every day helps, but you also need to change your clothes as regularly as you can to keep you smelling good. Unfortunately, you can't tell by looking at it if a piece of clothing is clean or dirty. For example, a t-shirt that you wore to school all day might not have an obvious spot or stain on it, but if you sniff the underarms? Pee-ooo. That's why it's best to keep your dirty clothes and your clean clothes far away from each other. That way you will be able to know the difference without doing the "sniff" test, which might not tell you for sure anyway.

Heading Out: Hair

Boys have it pretty easy when it comes to what people expect them to do with their hair. Regular shampooing (which might mean every day if you have oily hair or are very active) should just about do it.

Some boys use gel to make their hair stay in place. Some gels wash out easily, but some (especially ones that are wax-based) are much harder to get out. If you are going to use a wax-based gel or hair-molding product, you'll have to wash it out every night if you don't want to wake up in the morning with your hair looking like something from a horror movie.

Deodorant Works

Another possible weapon in your personal fight against "the smellies" is deodorant. Not everyone (even grown-ups) wears or needs deodorant, but if you want to try it, look for the type that says only "deodorant" and not "deodorant/ anti-perspirant." Anti-perspirant contains chemicals which actually block your sweat glands, which is not as healthy for your body. Some deodorants have a stronger smell than others, so you might have to try a few different kinds to find what smells best on you.

KNOW THE FACTS

Germs cannot be seen by your eyes so you have no way of knowing if they are on your hands. The warmth of your body combined with sweat allows germs to grow quickly.

If you have longer or particularly tangly hair, you can buy conditioner which you can use after you shampoo. You can also buy special shampoos for very dry hair (to keep you from having dandruff, which is when skin from your scalp flakes off and makes a mess) and shampoos for hair that is exposed to a lot of chlorine (for boys on a swim team).

The Ear From Which You Hear

The most important thing to remember about ears is: don't stick anything smaller than your elbow in them. That means no cotton tip swabs, no pen caps, and no paper clips! All these items can really hurt your ears if you stick them in too deep. If you are shampooing your hair regularly, that should be enough to keep your ears clean. Still, it

doesn't hurt to spend a little extra time with a washcloth, scrubbing behind your ears. If you have short hair, the dirt that builds up in that area can be very noticeable!

The wax you have in your ears is helpful: it keeps dirt from getting further down into your ear where it can do real damage. Although it might be tempting to pick at it, it's better to leave the wax alone and let it do its job.

If your ears feel clogged or you have trouble hearing, talk with your health care provider about things you can do to help get rid of some of the wax.

Putting Your Best Face Forward

The easiest way to take care of the skin on your face is to keep it clean. You can wash your face when you wash your hands, but try to use a gentle, non-perfumed soap. Don't use deodorant soap because it will leave a light film of deodorant on your face, and no one (no matter how smelly) needs deodorant on their face.

Another very common problem that boys have with the skin on their face is acne. Who gets acne? Almost everyone! Nine out of ten pre-teens and teenagers have to deal

The Expert Says

Have you seen how little kids hold their hands over their ears when something making a loud sound (like a fire engine with the siren blaring) goes by? They are smart because they know that loud sounds can hurt their ears. The headphones you wear when you play your iPod or stereo can also hurt your ears if it is too loud. Chances are that if other people can hear your music when you are wearing headphones it is too loud. When you are older, you'll be thankful that you turned down the volume!

WHAT'S THAT SPOT:
THE INS AND OUTS, UPS AND DOWNS OF ACNE

It might seem like some kind of mysterious plague, but there are some things you can do to tame the "zit monster."

● Washing your face can help reduce acne, but don't do it too often. If you wash your face more than three times a day or too harshly (you can't scrub your face like you scrub a dirty pan!) washing will irritate acne, not make it better.

- Don't pick! It can irritate your skin and cause an infection, and maybe even a permanent scar.

- You can buy creams at the drugstore to help with acne. Follow the directions and don't use more than the label says because benzoyl peroxide (the most common ingredient in over-the-counter acne creams) can be very irritating if you use too much.

- If you feel like your acne is out of control, talk with the adults in your life about going to a dermatologist, a doctor that specializes in skin.

- Despite how obvious your zit might feel to you, a lot of the time other people are too busy worrying about their own zits to think much of yours.

- After you finish the puberty process, you'll likely find that most (but not all) of your zit problems disappear. Just hang in there until then.

BOYS SAY:

I HAVE TO ADMIT THAT WHENEVER I GET A ZIT, I WANT TO POP IT. MY SISTER IS THE ONE WHO TOLD ME NOT TO DO THAT. SHE SAID THAT WILL MAKE IT WORSE, AND SHE WAS ACTUALLY RIGHT (FOR A CHANGE).

-Jerry, age 16

with it. Acne is caused when excess oil becomes trapped in your pores, combines with bacteria (i.e., germs) and dead skin cells and develops what we call a pimple.

Shaving

The first place you will probably have hair on your face is on your upper lip and chin. It will probably be just a little teeny amount (like the fuzz on a peach). You can remove this by shaving or by using a special depilatory powder made for men and boys who get "bumps" when they shave.

There is no medical reason to remove the hair from your face, but many boys find they are more comfortable without it. If you do decide to shave, when you first start you might only need to do it every few days because the hair won't grow that quickly.

The best way to learn about shaving is to talk to a male adult in your life (or an older brother) and get him to show you how to do it. For many boys, their first shave feels like an important part of becoming an adult.

Keeping Your Awesome Smile Looking Awesome

As you get older, the adults in your life will start expecting you to take more responsibility for things, including your oral hygiene (which is a fancy way of saying mouth care). And even though there is no longer an adult standing over you making sure you brush your teeth, now is the time to build good habits that will keep your teeth looking good for a lifetime.

You probably know someone (maybe a grandparent) who has lost their teeth and now has fake ones that they take out at night and keep in a cup by the bed! We know a lot more about dental care now than we did when they were young, so losing your teeth to tooth decay does not have to be a usual part of getting older.

Brushing is the most important thing you can do to keep your pearly whites, uh, pearly white. Besides brushing, flossing is another important thing you can do to help your teeth and gums stay healthy. Flossing removes food bits and bacteria from between your teeth. It helps avoid cavities and keeps your gums strong.

YOUR FIRST SHAVE

When you are ready for your first shave, it's best to get your dad, big brother, or another adult to walk you through it step by step, but here are some tips that will help the whole process go, um, smoother.

● First of all, choose a razor. There are 2 types of razors: electric and manual. An electric razor needs to be plugged in, or at least charged, while the manual types use old-fashioned arm movements. Manual razors are disposable so when the blade wears out, you usually just throw it away and get a new one. A lot of people think that electric razors do not shave as close as the disposable razors.

● If you choose a disposable razor, you will also need some type of shaving cream or gel to apply to your face before shaving. These creams and gels help lubricate your face and help reduce the risk of nicking or cutting your skin.

● The best time to shave is after taking a warm bath or shower to make sure your skin is hydrated and soft.

Now it's time to shave:

Step #1: Lather up! Apply shaving cream or gel.

#2. Go with the grain of your hair, not against it. Shaving against the grain (or upward) can cause rashes or red bumps.

#3. Don't rush and don't push down too hard with the razor. If you do, you're likely to cut your face. It's better to go over a part of the skin twice—lightly—than to press down hard. Ouch!

#4. Ask your mom or dad to get you an antiseptic styptic pencil. To use: dip the white pencil in water and then apply it to any nicks or cuts to stop bleeding immediately.

#5. Change razors or blades frequently. A dull blade can irritate your skin and cause rashes. You are also more likely to cut your face with a dull blade.

#6. After shaving, wash your face with soap and water. Then follow up your shave with a face lotion or moisturizing aftershave product. This will help prevent your skin from drying out. If you're heading outside, be sure to apply sunscreen with a sun protection factor (SPF) of at least 15 (higher if you have fair skin).

Congratulations on surviving your first shave. You'll soon be an expert since it is something many men do every day.

QUICK TIP

Shave with the grain! This means you should shave in the direction of how the hair grows on your face. Shaving against the grain can cause redness, rashes, razor burn, and ingrown hairs, which can be painful.

The Expert Says

Some foods are off-limits when you have braces. Ask your orthodontist before eating anything particularly sticky, such as caramels or gummy candy.

Avoid stinky breath. Brush your teeth.

Do I Have To Go? Boys and The Dentist

Although you can do a lot to help your teeth and mouth stay healthy at home, you also need a check-up and cleaning at the dentist's office every six months. Not all families have health insurance, and not all health insurance plans cover going to the dentist, but there are still ways to get dental care. Your school nurse can probably give you some ideas of how the adults in your life can make that happen.

Some people (not just kids) don't like going to the dentist. If this is the case for you, make sure you ask questions before you get to the dentist's office. Ask the adult who made the appointment for you why you have the appointment: are you only having your teeth cleaned or do you need something more done? Then, when you get to the dentist's office, before you open your mouth and say "ahhh," ask the dental hygienist or the dentist to explain exactly what is going to happen, step by step. Some procedures at the dentist's office might be uncomfortable, and the more information you have about when and how things might not feel so good, the more you can prepare yourself. A surprise birthday party might be a fun thing, but not a surprise in the dentist's chair!

LET'S BRUSH!

The foundation of all oral care is brushing your teeth. You probably think you're an expert, but for a quick review:

Step #1: Pick the right brush. A brush with bristles labeled "medium" or "hard" will be too tough on your gums and can actually contribute to gum disease! A toothbrush with worn out bristles won't get your teeth squeaky clean, so it works best if you replace your toothbrush every three to four months.

#2. Use toothpaste that contains fluoride, which, as you probably have heard on toothpaste commercials, is the ingredient that fights cavities.

#3. To start, brush the outside surfaces of your teeth (another way of saying this is the side that touches the inside of your cheek). Move the toothbrush back and forth, but in small strokes, and do a few teeth at a time. You will have to do it several times in each spot.

#4. When you are done brushing the outside of your teeth, brush the inside.

#5. Also brush the flat surfaces of your teeth (the chewing surface)

#6. Finally, brush your tongue. Your tongue can hold on to bacteria that can make your breath super-smelly!

#7. In order to really clean your teeth, you need to brush them for 2 to 3 minutes. Use a stop watch or the timer on the microwave to make sure you are brushing long enough.

#8. Don't forget to floss!

Tiny Little Train Tracks: The Drama of Braces

Lots of kids (and adults even) have braces. But even though braces are very common, sometimes even hearing that they MIGHT have to get braces makes boys sweat.

The most common reasons people need braces are because their teeth are crooked or because their upper and lower jaws are not the same size. Both of these problems can make it harder to care for your teeth. Braces don't just improve your smile: they can make your entire mouth healthier.

Getting braces is a perfect time to start taking more responsibility for your health. Ask your orthodontist about how you should care for your braces, what kind of foods you should avoid, and what you should do if part of your braces breaks off, gets bent, or irritates the inside of your mouth.

Meet Your Feet

Feet can be some of the smelliest parts of the body. This is because nearly everyone's feet sweat a lot. And since bacteria that can contribute to smelliness grow best in places that are not only damp, but also dark, you can see why taking off your shoes can sometimes be a frightening experience!

Avoid Those Athlete's Feet

Athlete's foot is easy to catch if you walk around barefoot where many other people walk around barefoot (like a school locker room, for example, which is probably where the nickname came from). The best way to avoid getting it is to buy special flip flops that you wear only in the locker room or public shower and to wash and dry your feet well every day.

Foot care is really no different than caring for any other part of your body, except that you have to wash your feet with a little more energy if you really want to get them clean. Make sure you separate each toe, because bacteria can get stuck in there and contribute to general smelliness. Make sure you dry your feet carefully afterwards and change your socks every day.

One common foot problem is called "athlete's foot," which is not caused by being an athlete. Athlete's foot is a fungus, and it can turn your feet into an itchy, smelly mess. If you have itchy feet and what looks like extra dry skin on the bottom of one or both of your feet (especially where your toes meet the ball of your foot) you might have athlete's foot. When you first get it, it can usually be treated with a special kind of medicine called an antifungal that the adult who is responsible for you can buy at almost any drugstore. It's important to treat athlete's foot right away because it can spread to even less fun parts of your body. Maybe you've heard of "jock itch?" Ewwww.

If the antifungal doesn't get rid of your athlete's foot, or if it spreads to the area on or near your toenails, you may need medicine you get from a health care provider to heal it up.

Athlete's foot is caused by a fungus. Up to 70% of the population will get it at some time in their lives.

A Good Smile = A Great First Impression

Chapter 3:

YOUR HEALTH AND YOUR BODY

Many boys find all the changes coming their way confusing. You might be worried that if you don't change at the same time – or in the same way – as other kids, that you might get teased or feel like a freak. It's true that it's not easy to be seen as different from the other kids around you, but there really isn't much you can do about it. Your body will develop when it's ready.

One thing that will help is to have a parent or other trusted adult to talk these things over with. There are also books like this one, as well as internet sites where you can find helpful information about your changing body and your changing life. You can even check out the resources section in the back of this book for some books and websites that might be helpful. Remember, though, that you're the expert on your own body and if something doesn't seem right or feels weird or painful

tell an adult you trust. The more you can learn about your body and the way it works, the better your lifelong relationship with your body will be!

Healthy Eating for Growing Boys

You might not want to hear this, but eating right—and we don't mean potato chips for breakfast, cookies for lunch, and candy for dinner—is really important at this time in your life. Your body is working hard to grow stronger and it really needs healthy food to do what it needs to do. Try to eat three healthy meals a day, starting with a nutritious breakfast. Eating fruits and vegetables at every meal will also help you keep at a weight that is good for you and will give you the energy you need to do all the fun things you want to do and even the boring stuff you need to do.

Healthy Foods For Boys On The Move

Here are some foods that are easy to grab when you are heading out the door and need a snack:

Granola Bar

Nuts

Apple

Navel Orange

Baby Carrots

Banana

Pretzels

Grapes

Crackers

Cheese Stick

Yogurt

Cereal

Graham Crackers

Peanut Butter on Celery

Toast

Mini Whole Wheat Bagel and Cream Cheese

Worried About Weight

Every time you turn on the television, you're likely to see an advertisement for some new diet pill, diet system, or contraption that will help people lose weight or keep them from getting fat. The reason there are so many of these systems, pills, and contraptions is because very few of them work in the long term. If you are concerned about your body size or weight, the answer is definitely not fad diets, pills, or starving yourself.

Instead, what you need is to get good nutrition and the right amount of calories to keep growing and keep going. Dieting makes food the enemy. Food isn't your enemy. Food is fuel and it should be fun. Learning to make good choices can be part of the fun.

Work with your body, not against it to keep healthy. Your body sends signals that say "I'm hungry" and it's important to know what hunger feels like for you. When you are eating because you're hungry, instead of just because you're upset or bored, it's easier to make healthier food choices.

Also, try to make food choices based on how you feel after you eat certain foods. For example, when you eat potato chips do you feel good afterwards? Do you feel like you have a lot of energy? Is it easier or harder to concentrate in school if you've had oatmeal for breakfast instead of a donut? Do you find the zit monster attacks after you've eaten oily foods? Does eating a banana before practice keep you from feeling hungry all the way through practice? What if you eat an chocolate bar?

BOYS SAY:

SPINACH IS ACTUALLY REALLY GOOD WHEN MY MOM COOKS IT WITH GARLIC AND OIL. I DIDN'T THINK IT WOULD BE BUT I TRIED IT AND I LIKED IT!

-Nathan, age 13

On the Go?
Make Better Fast Food Choices!

Fast food is easy, cheap, tasty, and it's everywhere. Since fast food isn't going to disappear anytime soon, you will need to take charge and make your own healthier choices as you get older:

● Don't think about "good" and "bad" foods. There are no specific foods that are good or bad, but some foods don't fuel your body very well. Many fast food choices are in this category.

● Fast food is highly processed; in other words, it's been a long time since it looked like the food that someone grew. Plus, because it comes from so far away and has been frozen, canned, or bagged, it takes a lot of preservatives and chemicals to make sure it still tastes good by the time it reaches your plate. These preservatives and chemicals make it harder for your body to use fast food as fuel.

● If there is a fruit option, consider taking the fruit.

● Sometimes a salad can be a good fast food choice, but don't overload with dressings, croutons, or other non-veggie toss-ins. Those don't add much nutrition.

● Just because the drink that comes with a fast food meal may have the word "juice" in it, that doesn't mean it's healthy. Watch out for sweeteners like high fructose corn syrup, which your body has a very hard time using for fuel.

● Think about training your taste buds. It's true that French fries taste great, but apples can taste pretty great, too, if you get into the habit of eating them.

● Make small changes first. If you usually eat an entire fast food meal and drink a large soda, start with carrying your own water bottle and eliminating the soda. After you've done that for a while, maybe switch it up from French fries to carrot sticks.

Sports: One Way To Work Your Muscles

As a little kid, you naturally moved around a lot. If you have a little brother or sister you might get tired just looking at them running around. However, as we get older, we spend more time in school and doing homework and less time (unfortunately!) moving our bodies. Sometimes the only time school age kids only get to jump and run around is a very short recess!

Team sports are one way to work your muscles, keep your body active, and have fun. But they definitely aren't the only way. Sometimes boys feel pressure to be good at sports. Sometimes this pressure comes from family members, parents, coaches, or friends. Sports might seem like the only way to be popular at your school. Playing a sport well is great, but your goal should be to enjoy yourself. Only a few boys will grow up to be pro athletes, but every boy can enjoy being a part of a team. Some reasons to play a team sport:

● Have fun.

● Get exercise and enjoy what your body can do.

● Learn skills (like how to pass and dribble but also self-confidence, self-discipline, and teamwork).

The Expert Says

Good sportsmanship— learning how to be both a good winner and a good loser—is an important part of playing sports.

BOYS SAY:

YOU HAVE TO TELL YOUR COACH WHEN YOU DON'T FEEL WELL. OTHERWISE HE DOESN'T KNOW TO PULL YOU OUT SO SOMEONE ELSE WHO FEELS OK CAN PLAY.

-Brendan, age 12

● Make friends.

● Release stress and pent up energy from sitting still all day.

Notice how "win every game" wasn't listed as a reason to play. Yes, winning is fun, especially compared to losing, but if there is too much emphasis placed on winning, sports actually become less fun. If the only thing that makes sports fun is winning, and only one team can win, that means only half the players get to enjoy it!

Would you and a bunch of your friends get together for a movie you knew half of you would hate? It would be a waste of time and money. Sports are the same way if the only goal is winning.

If losing is particularly hard for you, you can set personal goals for each game that don't depend on winning. For example, if you're an outfielder, you goal could be to catch 80% of the fly balls that come to you. If you struggle to support your team-mates, maybe your goal could be to find five things to compliment other players about.

Sometimes adults push kids too hard in sports. While pushing yourself a little can be good, pushing yourself and your

growing body too much can lead to permanent injuries. If you are feeling so much pressure that sports have lost some of their fun for you, it might be time to talk to your parents or the other adults in your life about this.

SPORTS SAFETY

Sports accidents do happen, but there are lots of things you can do to prevent them. One of the most important things you can do is to wear the right protective gear. Your head is super important since it's where your brain is kept. It's also one of the easiest parts of your body to protect: simply wear the helmet made for the sport you're playing. Have your coach adjust the helmet for you and always use the chin strap if the helmet comes with one. Otherwise your helmet might go flying one way and your head flying the other way at the exact moment when they should be sticking together!

For some sports, like soccer and football, you might also need to wear protective pads. Wear them, even if they're uncomfortable or you might be much more uncomfortable later.

Also very, very important: protecting your genital area. Two pieces of equipment can help protect your penis and testicles. These things are an athletic supporter (also known as a jock) and a cup. A cup is a hard piece of triangular plastic that, despite its name, looks nothing like a drinking cup. It goes inside your jockstrap and protects your genitals from direct blows, either from another player (for example, during a tackle or a tag play at home) or from equipment (the ball, a flying bat, etc.). Most kids call the whole thing together a cup. When you are in a hurry it might feel like wearing a cup and jock are too much bother. But if you've ever been hit by a ground ball that takes a funny hop, you know that even with a cup, it can be very painful. Without a cup you risk permanent damage. If other boys in the locker room give you a hard time about wearing a jock or a cup, tell them to mind their own business or do the final adjustments in the bathroom stall so that protection of your private parts is kept private.

Another very important way you can keep from being injured when you play sports is to warm up and stretch out before you start. Warming up and stretching give your muscles a chance to wake up and get

The Expert Says

Sometimes parents behave worse than the kids when it comes to sports. Try not to let it get to you if the adults around you are taking the game too seriously.

You win some, you lose some, but you always try again.

the blood flowing so you can perform at your best without getting hurt. There are special areas of your body you'll need to concentrate on stretching for different sports. Your coach should know all about this. If you are playing a sport that doesn't require teams or coaches (running or skateboarding, for example), you'll have to do your own research about stretching out. Someone more experienced in the sport may have some ideas or you can check your local library for books on the subject.

The final word of advice for staying safe when playing sports: don't play if you are hurt. It's easy to get caught up in the excitement of the final play or a close game. But playing when you are hurt can turn a small, not so serious injury into one that can give you problems for a long time. Since you're going to need your body for the rest of your life, it's not worth doing permanent damage! Anyone who asks you to play when you are actually injured is not respecting you or your body. You won't just be doing yourself a favor by taking yourself out of the game. You'll be helping your entire team be the best they can be.

Let's Get Moving

Team sports are definitely not the only way you can enjoy your body and build your health. If you don't like any team sports offered at your school or in your community, there are still individual sports that might be more your style. You could take up running on your own, or get your older cousin to teach you how to play tennis, for example. You can ride your bike or a skateboard or a scooter or a combination of all three (with protective equipment of course) and you'll be having so much fun you won't even know you're exercising! Dancing is fun movement as well, and so are some video games, the kind that make you jump, run in place, or dance around.

You can also go for walks, or hikes (a hike is basically a walk where there are a bunch of trees) or play the active games from when you were a little kid, like tag and red rover. Don't forget swimming on a hot day! Most big cities and even small towns have public pools and swimming is a good choice if you haven't been able to do a lot of movement for a while, because it's easy on the joints. Adding some movement into your day can really help you feel happier and less stressed while going through puberty. The mind and body connection is a real thing!

Performance Enhancements; Don't Risk It

Everyone wants to look good, but using steroids isn't the way to get there. All kinds of horrible things can happen to your body when you use steroids. Your testicles can shrink, you can grow breasts, you can lose your hair, get depressed, stop growing, or even die. Some of the effects of steroids are reversible. Some are not. Remember that a good body and better physical fitness is something you have to earn through practice and training, not through drugs. Don't risk your future just to have bulging biceps now!

Yawn! Boys and Sleep

When you were younger, your parents were more likely to enforce a strict bedtime. Now that you are older, you may still have a bedtime, but getting enough sleep is starting to become more and more your responsibility.

The average boy your age needs 10 hours of sleep a night in order to grow and be healthy. But you might need a little bit more or less than that. If you have trouble waking up in the morning,

SOME OTHER TIPS
FOR GETTING A GOOD NIGHT'S SLEEP

DO stay away from caffeine in the hours before you go to bed. You probably already know that certain types of soda contain caffeine, but did you know that chocolate does too?

DO avoid stimulating activities. For some boys this might mean not watching action or horror movies, reading exciting books, or playing "just until I reach the next level" of a video game, at least not right before bed. All these things are fun, but they aren't really relaxing.

DO avoid arguments or other things that might upset you emotionally right before you go to bed.

DO pack your bag and lay out your clothes for the next day. If you think you might forget something (like materials you need for a special project) write yourself a reminder note.

DO avoid screen time in general right before bed. It makes it hard for your brain to transition into the most restful type of sleep.

QUICK TIP

If you tend to wake up in the middle of the night remembering, "Oh, I can't believe I didn't tell Mrs. Walker I can't mow her lawn next week," keep a pen and paper by your bed so you can jot these things down.

KNOW THE FACTS

Wetting the bed doesn't mean you are lazy or a slob. It's something you can't help doing. The good news is that most kids who wet the bed eventually stop.

can't concentrate at school, or fall asleep during class, it might not be because you're bored. You just might not be getting enough sleep.

What if you have trouble getting to sleep? One of the things you can do to help yourself is to create a bedtime routine. If you do the same things every night, it will help your body recognize, "hey, it's time for sleeping now!" A bedtime routine might look something like: get in your pajamas, brush your teeth, say goodnight to your parents, read for 15 minutes, and then turn out the lights on another great day.

Wetting the Bed

Some boys (many more than you might think) have trouble with wetting the bed, even into their teen years. It is so common, in fact, that this problem has a special name: nocturnal (nighttime) enuresis. Most often this is caused by being a very deep sleeper, but other things can contribute to it as well, including a delay in the way your brain and bladder communicate with each other, a lower amount of a hormone that controls how much urine you make, or a smaller "functional" bladder, which means that while your bladder may be a normal size, when you sleep it sends a signal that it is full earlier than it needs to.

Many times nocturnal enuresis runs in families, so if you wet the bed, there is a good chance that someone you see at the family reunion did too. If you are wetting the bed, talk to an adult in your life about it. There are many simple things that can help with bedwetting, but it's best to get checked out by a doctor before you start any program of your own. This will make mornings (and sleepovers) a much more pleasant experience!

Chapter 4:

YOUR CHANGING BODY IN THE OUTSIDE WORLD

As you get older, parents and teachers (and therefore, kids) talk a lot more about grades. Some schools give marks like "satisfactory" or "needs improvement" in earlier years, but by third grade, many schools have switched to the more common A, B, C (well, you know the rest...) system. This makes a lot of kids nervous because they seem more like "real" grades, something that will count and cause them trouble in the future if they don't do well.

Sometimes boys put lots of pressure on other boys to NOT do well in school because they don't think it's "cool" to get good grades. If this is happening to you, talk with an adult you trust about it. This can be a hard situation to handle, especially if the kids who are teasing you about your good grades are old friends. You've probably heard the term "peer pressure" (pressure other kids put on you to be, act, or dress like them) and this is a perfect example. See Chapter 7 for tips on dealing with peer pressure. One thing an adult can do is help you figure out ways to meet other kids who like to study and don't mind being thought of as "smart." Also, ask your teacher for help in keeping your grades private. Teachers sometimes like to praise their best students in front of the other kids, but he or she might not know about the trouble it is causing you!

> **Learning begins when you say, "I don't know."**

A QUIZ:
WHAT DO YOU KNOW ABOUT GRADES?

True or false.
If you get a good grade it means you've learned a lot. If you get a bad grade, you haven't learned anything.

Answer: False!
Grades are one way of showing how much you've learned, but they aren't perfect. Sometimes a lower grade in a hard subject means you actually learned more than a higher grade in a subject that's easy for you.

True or false.
Even smart kids can sometimes get bad grades or have a hard time in school.

Answer: True!
The grades that you see on your report card do NOT mean "dumb" or "smart." There are lots of kinds of intelligence. Even if school is not that easy for you, you can bet that you have special skills somewhere else, even if you haven't discovered them yet.

True or false.
If you are getting a bad grade in a subject, just give up, quit school, and move to Australia, there's nothing you can do to change it.

Answer: False!

Just because you are getting low grades in a subject, it doesn't mean you aren't good at that subject, or that your grade in that subject has to stay low. Talk to your teacher about what you need to do to bring the grade up.

True or false.

You should like all subjects equally. If you don't like math and spelling the same amount, there is something very, very wrong with you.

Answer: False!

It's normal to have some subjects that you like and some subjects that you don't. After all, haven't grown-ups been asking you "What's your favorite subject?" since kindergarten. In fact, if you do the homework for the classes you like least first, you can use the homework for the classes you like more as a reward for yourself!

Multiple Choice

If you are having trouble in school, you can get help from:

a. Your teacher after school

b. Summer camp

c. After-school study groups

d. Your neighborhood library

e. An adult at home

f. The guy who feeds the lions at the zoo

Yes, you guessed it, every one but "F." And you could ask the guy at the zoo, but please don't distract him while he's feeding the lion. If he ends up being cat food he won't be able to be much help to you.

> I don't think much of a man who is not wiser today than he was yesterday.
> —ABRAHAM LINCOLN

Homework and Study Skills

There isn't room in this book for all the information we could include about study skills. If you are interested in learning more about how to study, your school librarian can point you to entire books on the subject. However, there are a few simple things you can do right now to make your study time more effective:

● The very first thing you need to know about homework is what your homework is. Keep a small notebook with all your assignments in it and you'll never be wondering what is due when. Unless you lose the notebook, that is, so try not to lose that notebook!

● Set aside a special time to study every day. For some kids, right after they get home from school works. Other kids need a break and prefer to dig into their books after they get something to eat and have some time to relax or do other chores.

● Find a quiet place to study. If home doesn't work, try your school or community library.

● Don't wait until the night before a project is due to start it. If you have any questions or don't understand something you won't have time to get the answers you need.

● Having trouble concentrating while you're doing your homework? Set a timer on your phone or the clock on the microwave to help you work your "sticking to it" muscles. If you hate math, promise yourself that if you do nothing but your math homework for 30 minutes, you can take a break or move on to something more fun.

Getting Along With Teachers

If you ever want to get a grown-up talking, ask them to tell you about their favorite teacher. Then ask them about their least favorite teacher. Never ask these questions if you have somewhere to be soon; those questions usually lead to very long stories!

The fact that grown-ups will talk so fondly about things that happened so long ago might remind you how important teachers are to ALL kids. Hopefully, you've already had a few teachers that you really liked. Probably you've had some teachers that you didn't like as much. This is very normal.

Although you might not have a lot (or any) choice about who

QUICK TIP

This is the time to start keeping a little notebook (or a big, huge notebook if you need it) where you write down all your assignments and check them off when they're done. You'll be able to have more fun hanging out after school if you can look at your notebook and see you've got everything taken care of! You can also use your assignment notebook to remind you of the things you need to take to school in the morning.

your teachers are right now, you do have choices about what to do when you have a difficult teacher/student situation.

If a teacher is getting on your nerves, it might be tempting to think, "you're not the boss of me." Except for, well, when you are at school, they are the boss of you. If you are having trouble getting along with a teacher, try and think of it as a chance to learn a very important grown-up skill. Just like a boy might have to learn from a teacher he might not like, grown-ups sometimes have to work for bosses they don't get along with. It might not be easy for you, but there are some things you can try to help your school-life go more smoothly.

One thing you can do if you are having trouble getting along with a teacher is to try and give it a little time. Especially at the beginning of the year, teachers have a lot to do with setting up their classrooms and getting books and supplies ready. You might find they act differently when things settle down, further into the school year. Since every boy and every teacher is different, it might take you and the teacher time to figure each other out.

If things don't seem to be getting better, talk to an adult you trust. This can be a parent, family friend, etc. You are probably already talking to someone your own age. This is good for letting off steam, but other kids might not have the experience to help you completely sort out the problem.

If none of this helps, ask an adult if they would help you set up a meeting with the teacher. Sometimes just talking about the problem directly, especially if you have an adult who understands you and can help you explain yourself if you get stuck, can really help a lot.

As you go through school, you will have some teachers who you feel really close to and some that you can't wait to say goodbye

QUICK TIP

While it's normal to have some teachers you like and some you don't, if your relationship with your teacher is making it hard for you to learn, there are some things you can do to improve the situation.

● Since you can only change your own behavior, look at that first. Do you show up on time? Do you do your homework? Are you respectful? Do you ask questions when you don't understand something? If you answered no to any of these questions, look to changing your own behavior first.

Reach out to the teachers you admire.

● If your teacher has some "pet peeves" (behaviors that particularly annoy or bother them) getting along might be as simple as not doing those things!

● If you need to bring up an issue with a teacher, do it after class. Most teachers are more relaxed one-on-one than when they are dealing with a whole classroom of kids.

● Sometimes it might feel like the problem is the teacher, when the real difficulty is that the subject they teach is one you don't like or that you have a hard time with. If the class is hard for you, make sure the teacher knows you are doing your best.

● Talk to your parents about the problem. They can help you set up a meeting with the teacher where you can talk about the problem.

to at the end of the year. If you can figure out how to learn from all different types of teachers, you will have some very important life skills that will help you a lot in later years.

Extracurricular Activities

Sometimes boys think that if they aren't good at sports, they can't be a part of things. But that's just not true. Even if you don't like the sports teams at school, there are many other activities you can get involved in. Plus, school is not the only place to be on teams! Sometimes you can find different kinds of teams or learn how to play different sports at your community recreational center or through camps or clubs. And most schools, especially as you get older, have many different kinds of opportunities for having fun and making friends and learning what you are good at.

If your school doesn't offer an activity you'd like, maybe you can suggest it. If you can't find any groups or clubs you like at your school, often community centers, youth centers, and religious organizations have activities for boys as well.

Non-Sport Activities

Don't like sports? No problem! Try:

● Writing for the school paper.

● Taking pictures for the yearbook.

● Playing chess on the school chess team or in the school chess club.

● Singing in the choir.

● Acting in (or making sets or designing costumes for) the school play.

● Running for student government.

● Helping plan dances or other fun events (many schools have a social committee for things like this).

● Learning about running and fixing electronic equipment in the AV club.

● Learning about another culture and language in (for example) a Spanish club.

● Performing a stand up comedy routine in the school talent show.

● Playing a musical instrument.

● Volunteering as a tutor to someone who needs help.

● Working behind the scenes for a sports team keeping score or helping the coach.

Getting an After-School Job

Getting a job after school is a great way to expand your horizons and make some money at the same time. While you may be too young yet to hold a job in a store or restaurant (two of the more common after-school jobs for teenagers) there are plenty of jobs out there for someone your age. For example, you could mow lawns or shovel snow. You could babysit for your neighbors. You could walk dogs or water plants for people who are on vacation.

Two of the most important things you will learn from having an after-school job are to take responsibility for the work you do and to do your work the best you can. You'll also learn how hard you have to work to make money, which will help you appreciate all that your parents have given you. Finally, you'll have money to go to the movies and do the other things you like to do.

Saving Money (a.k.a. Taking Personal Responsibility for Buying The Things You Want for Yourself)

One of the best things about having a small job such as babysitting or moving lawns is that it makes it possible for you to save some money. Of course, you'll want to put some of the money you make in a special account for when you're ready to go to college or buy your first car, but you can save money for smaller things you need or want as well.

It's easy to spend other people's money. You just walk into the store, pick out what you want, and poof, mom pulls out her credit

Instead of spending your money on candy and other small stuff, save the money you earn from your job to buy something big you really want. If you save up enough, you'll be the envy of your friends when you buy your first car.

card and it's yours. However, when you've taken the time to earn that money yourself you'll likely have a different feeling about your purchase. When you save for something you want, you develop an understanding of what it really costs to buy that expensive pair of shoes or electronic gadget. You'll likely discover that it's not just money, it's all that sweat it took to get that money. Is it worth the effort of mowing 25 lawns to get that specific pair of shoes you wanted? The answer depends on your personal experience. You might love and value the shoes even more, or you might decide the shoes were not worth all that!

Going to College

You might already be thinking about college, or you might not yet. It's still early so try and keep your mind open to all the possibilities. Even if no one in your family has been to college, or your family doesn't have a lot of money, it is still possible for you to get a higher education. There are a lot of options such as scholarships and other types of financial aid. You can also spend your first two years at a community college which is usually much less expensive than going to a private four-year school. While college isn't for everyone, going to college

KNOW THE FACTS

A college graduate can be expected to earn more than a million dollars more over the course of his life than someone with just a high school diploma.

77

can open your eyes to some of the less obvious careers out there. Plus, a good education can help you not only get a job that pays more money, but also to have many more jobs to choose from.

However, a college degree is not the only way to get a job you enjoy. There are some jobs that require specialized training, but not college. Some jobs (such as being a plumber) require you to complete an apprenticeship. An apprenticeship is where you spend time learning from an experienced person in that profession, but not in a formal classroom setting. Generally, jobs that require apprenticeships let you use your body more than an office-type job such as an accountant or writer. So if you are the type of boy who likes to be outside a lot or likes to use his hands to build or fix things, you might want to investigate the types of jobs you can learn through hands-on training. Your adult self will thank you for taking the time to explore all the post-high school opportunities available to you before making a decision that has the power to effect the rest of your life.

The best way to predict your future is to create it.

Considering Your Future

One of the benefits in getting involved in fun activities outside of regular schoolwork is that you can learn more about what you're good at and what you like to do. These things might have nothing to do with your regularly scheduled classes. You can also meet more adults and get some ideas about jobs you might like to consider for a future career.

Besides extracurricular activities, there are lots of other ways to find out about different jobs. If you think you might be interested in, for example, growing tulips for a living, but you live in Arizona and don't know anyone who grows anything but a cactus now and then, try finding a book about the subject. Or ask an adult or teacher to help you find some information online. Also, some colleges include career information for younger students on their websites.

Even if you don't have any career ideas floating around in your head at this point, don't worry. While it's helpful to be thinking about what talents you have and what you can be involved in that will nurture those talents, doing well in school and participating in extracurricular activities is a good start.

It's great to have a really certain idea about what you would like to do for work when you get older, but it's also okay to change your mind a lot! There are lots of adults who still aren't sure what they want to be when they grow up!

BOYS SAY:

I ALWAYS THOUGHT I WANTED TO BE AN LAWYER... UNTIL I GOT TO COLLEGE THAT IS. THEN I HAD THE CHANCE TO TAKE A CLASS IN DIPLOMACY AND I DECIDED I WANTED TO WORK FOR THE AMERICAN EMBASSY. I DIDN'T EVEN KNOW THAT JOB EXISTED WHEN I WAS IN HIGH SCHOOL!

William, age 21

Chapter 5:

CHANGES AT HOME

You might have noticed this book mostly talks about the "adults in your life" or "adults at home" instead of using the more specific "parents." That's because not all boys are raised by their parents. Some boys are raised by a single parent, grandparents, two moms, two dads, in foster families, blended families, by aunts and uncles, and combinations of the above. We want those boys to understand that this book is for them, too. Every family is unique and different from every other family. What's important is that you have an adult in your life who you can trust.

**Offer to call or
text message
your parents to
check in when
you are out with
friends. Always
have a plan for
getting out of
unsafe situations.**

What Do These People Want From Me?

The process of going from being a kid to being an adult is mostly about taking more and more responsibility for more and more bits of your life. This goes on until you are managing most of your everyday choices yourself, or until you become, as the saying goes, "the boss of you." The truth is you're never totally the boss of you. We live in a complex society. Even when you are an adult there will be some people (your boss at work, the police, your girlfriend) who will have the power to enforce consequences if you don't follow the rules. Of course, your boss probably won't give you a bedtime or tell you what kind of TV shows you can watch and your girlfriend probably won't insist you eat your vegetables before you have dessert (but you never know).

Responsibility and You

Most of the common everyday conflicts that happen between boys in the transition between childhood and adulthood and their parents centers around issues of responsibility. A parent thinks a boy isn't responsible enough, for example, to make choices about seeing a certain movie or going to a certain party. The boy thinks he definitely is. Sound familiar? Of course, the opposite can be true as well. A parent thinks a boy is old enough to mow the lawn and take out the trash; the boy thinks that's too much responsibility for someone his age.

Some conflict between teens and pre-teens and the adults in their lives is normal, even healthy. The job of kids as they get older is to separate from their parents until they are independent enough to live on their own. The job of parents is to give kids loving guidance, set limits, and make sure they are actually ready to live on their own when the time comes.

You've probably noticed you don't have control over what your parents do. But you do have control over what you do. One big step you can take towards getting to do more things you want to do is to work on building your parents' trust in you. The easiest way to do this is to do WHAT you say you are going to do WHEN you say you're going to do it. If you agree to help your little brother with his homework after school, take the time to help, even if you'd really rather watch something (anything even) on TV. If your parents give you a time to be home, make sure you're there on time, even if everyone else has a later curfew and is bugging you to stay just a "few more minutes." If you say you are going to a party, be at that party, not somewhere else, unless you call and get permission first.

THE CARE AND FEEDING OF PARENTS:

HOW TO TALK SO THEY'LL LISTEN

What else can you do to help your relationship with your parents go better? Lots of things. For example:

● If you end up in a mess, confess early and ask for help. You are going to make mistakes sometimes. Most parents remember this. Covering up a mess almost always guarantees a bigger disaster in the end.

● Tell them how you're feeling. It may seem like they can read your mind, but they can't.

● Treat your parents like people. They are! Try talking about something they are interested in. (Hint: it's probably not video games.)

● Try not to roll your eyes at them. Eye-rolling often drives even the calmest parents wild.

● If you are in the middle of a discussion that is turning into an argument, ask to take a break and calm down.

● Listen to your parents. Ask questions. Show that you are trying, at least, to understand their point of view.

● Pick your battles. You don't care about everything equally, so try to give in without a big discussion on some things you care less about. Your parents will listen more closely when you bring up an issue if they don't feel like you are always complaining about every rule they make.

The average curfew for a 13-year-old boy is 9pm weeknights and 10pm on weekends.

Curfews and Other Rules

Curfews are often a hot button issue for adults and kids. This is a perfect time for you to work on the art of the compromise. Sometimes parents will let you come in later if they know you are safe when you are out. Work with them on what you would do if, for example, you got to a party and there wasn't an adult there, or kids were drinking. If they know you have a way to stay safe, they'll feel better about being flexible with your curfew.

If you and your parents are constantly fighting about rules in the house, ask for more details about their expectations. For example, a common rule adults make is "kids must keep their rooms clean." Well, to you, "clean" might mean "no fungus growing on the carpet." To your parents, "clean" might mean that your bed is made every day and that you vacuum twice a week.

Chores

Most families have expectations about how kids help out. This might include small things like clearing the table after dinner, or bigger things like housecleaning, or even helping with a family farm or store. These expectations can be a source of conflict between boys and parents, especially if boys feel like helping around the house cuts into their social time too much.

Luckily, there are some ways to negotiate about chores so that both parents and boys will feel like they are getting some of their needs met.

If you and your parents are feeling frustrated around the subject of chores, ask for a family meeting to discuss things. Prepare for the meeting beforehand by thinking about what areas need to change and what compromises seem reasonable to you. It might help to come armed with some additional areas of chores that you might be willing to do to help the house run smoothly in exchange for having less responsibilities in another area. For example, if helping with dinner puts too much pressure on you to get home quickly after sports practice, maybe you could ask what you could help with in the morning instead.

If your parents complain that you are not doing a good job at the chores you are doing, ask for more details about exactly what they expect to be done. Try making

BOYS SAY:

I GET AN ALLOWANCE FROM MY PARENTS BASED ON THE NUMBER OF CHORES I ACCOMPLISH EACH WEEK. IF I WANT TO HAVE MORE MONEY, I HAVE TO DO MORE CHORES. THAT SEEMS FAIR TO BOTH ME AND MY PARENTS.

Dwayne, Age 13

an actual list: break the chore down to its smallest parts and check each of them off as you do them.

Oh Brother (And Oh Sister): The Art Of Being Friends With Siblings

Brothers and sisters can be really fun, but that doesn't mean it's easy for siblings to get along. Some things that might help:

It is common for younger kids to feel like their older siblings get to "have all the fun" and do whatever they want. Older brothers and sisters often think that the baby of the family gets more than his or her share of attention. Try and remember that there are good things and bad things about whenever you came into your family, and most times these things are pretty even in the end.

Don't be confused if you feel both proud AND jealous of your siblings, sometimes even at the exact same time. If you are feeling jealous of what your siblings have done, remind yourself that you have special skills and talents that they don't have.

Did you know you can make "just between siblings" rules? For example, if you and your brother have run into problems when you tease each other, you could agree never to tease each other where other (non-family members) can hear. Or you can agree never to tease each other about certain things.

Older brothers and sisters can really help make this time in your life easier if you ask them. If you're the oldest, remember to be there for your younger siblings when they get to be your age.

You might not believe it now, but your brothers and sisters may be the best friends you have throughout your life. If you invest in your relationship with them now, it will really pay off later on.

QUICK TIP

If you are sharing a room with a sibling, keep one small section (even if it is part of a closet or the top of your desk) as yours. Having a private spot to keep private things can help you feel safe.

Chapter 6:

YOUR CHANGING FEELINGS AND FRIENDS

As if it isn't enough that your body and your feelings are changing, many boys find this is an age where they have to make a whole new group of friends!

Sometimes this happens because you are going to a bigger middle school and the kids you used to hang out with are in different classes and have a different schedule than you. Sometimes the crowd that you hung out with when you were younger starts doing things you don't like and you need to find a new crowd to hang out with. Sometimes you just find that your interests have changed and you don't have anything in common with your old friends anymore. Whatever the reason, making new friends can be scary but ultimately rewarding.

A FEW TIPS FOR MAKING NEW FRIENDS:

Some friendships just happen, but more often you need to make a special effort to find good friends. Here are a few ways to start.

Being friendly (waving to people, smiling, cracking jokes with them) is a good beginning. Be interested in your new potential friend. Ask him questions about his likes and dislikes, how things are going for him, or what kinds of things he likes to do after school.

One way of really cementing a friendship is by doing things together besides watching TV and playing video games. Activities that don't require you to interact much can't help you get to know your friend very well. Try going to the park, playing a board game, or building something together instead.

If you want to change crowds, you can sometimes start by making a few new friends. Eat lunch with someone new, chat with him between classes. You can find things you have in common this way.

The Expert Says

Trust is one of the most important traits a new friend can offer. If you can't trust someone, he can't be a good friend to you.

If you are having trouble finding and keeping good friends, you might try making a list of the qualities (for example, sense of humor, likes to do the same things, even-tempered) that you are looking for in a friend. Look around to see who has those qualities: it might be someone you weren't expecting!

Friendship Skills

Although in some ways it's natural to be a good friend to someone you care about, there are skills that can make being a good friend easier.

For example, everyone makes mistakes in friendships. We say something that we don't mean when we are tired or angry, or we let our good-natured teasing go too far. One of the surest ways to keep a friendship growing strong is to apologize when you do something to hurt your friend's feelings. It works best if you don't say, "I'm sorry but…" and then go on to explain to the person why they are wrong. That's not really an apology! It's a way of keeping an argument going!

Another thing that helps keep a friendship growing is talking through disagreements before they get really big. If a friend borrows your baseball glove and doesn't bring it back when he promised to, it's better to mention it the first time he does it and not wait until the tenth time and blow up. He might not even know that it bothers you until you tell him.

"The only way to have a friend is to be one."

— RALPH WALDO EMERSON

Being a good listener is one of the most important friendship-building skills you can have. Sometimes it can be hard to listen. Your friend might want to talk about a movie that you thought was stupid. Interrupting with "booooorrring" might make your friend laugh the first time, but it won't feel great when he does it back to you. If you make the extra effort to pay attention to what your friend has to say, you might become more interested in the conversation and decide the movie wasn't so stupid after all!

Dating and Romance

Around puberty, boys often start looking at girls a bit differently. Some start wondering if everything about talking to girls has changed. It doesn't have to. You can still be great friends with a girl. If you catch any slack about that, either ignore it, or just say "yes, she's my friend and she's a girl," over and over until the teasers get bored and find someone else to bother.

This is a time in your life when you are exploring relationships and getting to know yourself better. While you might sometimes have romantic feelings or crushes, don't put pressure on yourself to start that part of your life too soon. If you are interested in dating or "going out with" someone, work on being friends first. Try different fun activities where you can get to know that person. Going to the moves, which is a very typical first date, doesn't allow for much talking so it might not be the best way to get to know someone. In fact, it will be less pressure for both of you if you go out with a few other friends (they can be on a date or not) for a group activity.

If you feel a lot of pressure from your friends to jump into dating before you are ready, it can help to make at least a few friends who are running at your same speed when it comes to romantic relationships.

QUICK TIP

Don't assume that someone doesn't want to be friends just because they don't say hi to you. The person could be really shy and afraid to make the first move.

95

BOYS SAY:

PULL UP YOUR PANTS, MAN. IT'S NOT COOL.

-Lincoln, age 17

Dress for Success

When you were little your mom probably picked out your clothes for you. Now that you're older, it can be fun to express yourself with your clothes and to see how far you can take your personal style. It can be really fun to experiment with different fashions and see what looks best on you. There are a lot of different types of fashion out there and that means every boy should be able to find a style that suits him.

For example, if you opt for jeans with a ton of rips in them or try that style where the jeans are so big that they actually fit you somewhere around your ankles, you are sending a message to those around you. Similarly, wearing a suit and tie on a daily basis also sends a message. The trick is to match your clothes with the message you want to send. You might think your style says "I'm too cool to care that I'm wearing a stained thermal shirt" but to everyone else it might be saying that you're lazy or careless, even if you're not.

When you get dressed in the morning, ask yourself "what do my clothes say about me?" If you think people might be getting the wrong message, change the channel by changing your style. You'll likely discover that when you dress for success, success comes and seeks you out.

Your Self-Image

One of the hardest things about being a growing boy with a changing body and changing feelings is that all these changes can make you feel unsure about who you are. Every day, ads on television, online, and in magazines tell you what a "real man" is, and you might wonder how you will measure up. First, it's important to remember that there is no type of man that is "unreal." But still, what other people think about you, the judgments they make based on how you look or what clothes you wear, can hurt a lot.

This is why it's important to work on your own self-image so that you can feel good about who you are, inside and outside. If you are struggling to feel positive about who you are, ask your friends and trusted adults in your life what your best qualities are. Why do they like being your friend? What is unique about you? How does your presence make the world a better place?

Remind yourself about these things when you're feeling down about not having a perfectly zit-free face, didn't get the part you wanted in the school play, or don't have the latest expensive sneakers.

Chapter 7:

STAYING SAFE IN THE REAL AND VIRTUAL WORLDS

The internet can be a pretty amazing place. You can communicate with friends and far-away family members, learn more about your favorite hobbies and interests, play games, learn random trivia tidbits to impress your friends, and watch a lot of videos of cats doing funny things.

The number one thing you need to always remember and never forget is that nothing you post or share in the cyber world (or through any kind of electronic connection) is ever really private.

Before you send that text or photo out there, ask yourself: would I be okay with everyone in the whole world knowing what I am saying right now or seeing this picture? Not just the person I am sending this to, but everyone? My family? My teachers? My principal? Total strangers?

Even what you post on supposedly anonymous apps or videos that "disappear" after they are watched doesn't always stay private. Anything can be screenshot or screen-capped, and once it's out there, it's out there forever. You lose control completely. Anyone can share it, and anyone can pass it around. You've made a digital trail that can continue to follow you long after you've hit send.

The trail doesn't have to be made on purpose to cause you problems: the person you share a photo with can be a best friend who would never ever betray you or share the photo without your permission. But what happens if they lose their phone at school and the photo gets into someone else's hands? Even if it's just a goofy photo of you waking up in the morning with hair sticking straight up, you might not want everyone in the world to see it.

Also remember: almost everyone you meet online is a stranger. And the trustworthy adults in your life have warned you about talking to strangers, right? If someone you don't know in real life contacts you online and wants to meet with you, tell a trusted

Check out www.isafe.org for more internet safety tips.

adult. Online, anyone can say they are a kid or even use someone else's photos to make a fake profile.

Also, think carefully about sharing personal information such as locations (for example, "checking in" on different social media sites) or the fact that you're home alone ("Watching scary movie while fam is out, jumping at every noise LOL") to everyone with a phone or an Internet connection.

Give Yourself a Break

The beauty of having the world at your fingertips through a smartphone is that you can reach out to anyone you need to, whenever you need to.

The drawback is...the world can also reach you!

Especially as you approach your teen years, when you're building your own social groups outside of your family, social contact becomes more of the focus of your daily life, almost like a job. A fun job, but still a job. If you're on your phone 24/7 and available all the time, that's like working around the clock. Even brain surgeons have days off, right?

Here are a few ways you can take charge of your digital life instead of letting it take charge of you:

● Make sure you have real conversations, not just text conversations, with your friends. With text, you have time to think through every interaction, and consider exactly how it will be understood and what it says about you. But real-time, real-life conservations are more spontaneous and just as fun!

● Set your phone to airplane mode at night, or use the "do not disturb" function. If you're worried about missing an emergency call, you can set the "do not disturb" to allow incoming calls from your favorites or from the same caller within a short time period, like three minutes.

● Have "screen-free" days once in a while. You deserve to have some personal time. You do not have to be instantly available to everyone you know, all the time. Maybe being occasionally unavailable will lend you an air of mystery!

● Experiment with going to a concert or a movie or out with friends without taking photos or posting about it on social media. It's a different kind of experience, and you might enjoy it in a different way.

Peer Pressure

The biggest thing to remember about peer pressure is that whatever "it" is, everyone is not doing it. Resisting peer pressure can be hard. Some boys say it is one of the most difficult things about these in-between years. Here are some tricks you can use when dealing with other kids who want you to do something you don't want to do:

● Practice saying "no" when it isn't super important. This will help you be thought of as someone who doesn't just go along with the crowd. Often kids will stop pressuring you if they know you aren't going to give in because it makes them look silly.

● Physically remove yourself from situations in which you feel pressure to do something you don't want to do. If you know that the boys in the corner at recess are going to be plotting their next wedgie victim and you don't want to be part of the mean wedgie-giving gang, don't walk by them. Take the long way around.

● Ask a good friend or a trusted adult to help you brainstorm ways to deal with things kids say when they are trying to get you to

do something you don't want to do. Make up flash cards to carry around with you to remind you what to say.

● Have a "peer pressure" buddy. If your friend sees you struggling to say "no" to something everyone else seems to be saying "yes" to, he can jump in with, "Well, I'm not going to do it either." Having one person on your side feels totally different than going it alone. Make sure you return the favor for your friend!

● The biggest thing that can help you deal with peer pressure is feeling confident in yourself and in your abilities. As you get involved and find things you are good at, you will feel stronger to resist the pressure because you know more about who you are and what you want in life.

Bullying and Teasing: How To Protect Yourself

Bullying and peer pressure are two different things, although sometimes they can feel pretty much the same: basically bullying is peer pressure amped up to the highest degree. If another kid says you won't be cool if you don't smoke a cigarette with them, that's peer pressure. If another kid threatens to beat you up if you don't smoke a cigarette, that's bullying.

Bullying can be more than physical threats. Someone can bully you by saying really mean things about you, a lot, over time. They can threaten to tell a secret that will cause you problems if it gets out. Even writing mean words on your locker is a form of bullying. If you are getting bullied, it might feel hopeless but there are things you can do to protect yourself.

First of all, remember that getting bullied is never your fault. You have to really believe this. It's in the best interest of the bullies to make you ashamed of who you are, or whatever they want to bully you about.

Tell your parents, teachers, or a trusted adult right away if you are being bullied. If that adult won't do something, tell another adult. Keep telling adults until you get some help.

Wherever most of the bullying is happening, try to spend less time alone in those physical spaces. If you're getting bullied at school, ask a friend to walk to class with you each day. If you're getting bullied in your neighborhood, walk home with a bunch of kids instead of by yourself. If you are getting bullied on the bus, sit right up front near the bus driver or near a patrol instead of toward the back.

Find support for whatever it is that the bullies are teasing or bullying you about. For example, if you are getting teased for getting good grades, make sure you hang out with other brainy kids. There is often safety in numbers and as an added bonus you can see how they handle any negative attention they might get.

Be an Army of One

Bullies often get away with their behavior because no one is willing to step forward and say "Stop!" Studies have shown that if even one kid stands up for a kid who is being bullied, that the bullying often stops or become much less frequent.

You can be that kid who steps forward and says "Stop." Yes, it takes bravery. Yes, it could mean you draw some negative behavior on yourself, but it can also mean that someone's life gets so much better just because of you, and that's one of the best feelings in the world.

Also, someday, you might be looking for someone to step up and say "Stop" when some bully is bothering you. That's much more likely to happen if you've done the same for someone else.

Personal Safety

Bullying and peer pressure are not the only ways that kids can get hurt, and that's why it's important to understand the boundaries between you and other people.

You probably already know the message that your body is yours and that no one (except sometimes a doctor in the

BOYS SAY:

I TRY TO BE FRIENDLY TO EVERYONE, WHETHER THEY ARE POPULAR OR NOT. THAT WAY, YOU ALWAYS KNOW SOMEONE WHEN YOU GET TO A CLASS OR WALK DOWN THE HALL. YOU ARE NEVER ALONE.

-Andrew, age 15

doctor's office) has the right to touch you in your private areas, which are the areas usually covered by a bathing suit. This isn't just true for strangers. It's true for everyone in your life. Even if a person is someone your family knows, or a relative, or someone who is very nice to you or pays special attention to you, they still don't have the right to touch you in these areas.

If someone does try to touch you in a way that doesn't feel right to you, it's not your fault. It's never your fault when an adult doesn't respect your private areas, even if they say it is. Even if they beg you not to tell anyone, tell your parents or another adult you trust as soon as possible.

There are some things you can do out in the world that will help you stay safe. You probably already know you shouldn't talk with strangers or get into a car with adults you don't know. But now that you are older, there are other rules you should know as well.

Always ask to see the badge or identification card of anyone (like a police officer or a gas repair person) who comes to the door. Always check with your parents to see if they are expecting them before you open the door; you can even check the badge through the peephole, that's what it is made for! When in doubt, don't open the door. Just tell whoever it is to come back again some other time.

Cyberbullying

Cyberbullying is any kind of bullying that takes place using electronic technology like cell phones, computers, or any other device you can use to get online. It is not that different from everyday in-person bullying, but at times it can be even more harmful because:

⬤ Cyberbullying can take place anytime, any place. You don't have to be anywhere near the person bullying you to feel scared or threatened.

⬤ People who engage in cyberbullying don't have to see the face of the person they are hurting; this can help bullying behavior get out of control even more quickly.

⬤ Online, it's easy to post anonymous information or hide behind a fake profile so bullies don't have to take responsibility for their actions.

So, what can you do about cyberbullying?

Like bullying in real life, being the victim of cyberbullies is never your fault. But you can do certain things to protect yourself and the people you care about.

⬤ Say something. If someone is threatening you, spreading rumors about you, sharing your private information, forwarding your messages, or engaging in cyberbullying, tell a trusted adult right away. Information and gossip spreads fast on the Internet, so acting quickly is important.

⬤ Protect personal information. This means not letting yourself be pressured into sharing any photos or information that you don't want to share or that you wouldn't want shared with the whole world!

⬤ Don't participate in cyberbullying yourself in any way, and do your part to protect other kids. If someone posts something harmful or private about someone, don't "like" it or share it. If you know someone has created a fake profile and is using it to bully, report it or tell an adult you trust.

Chapter 8:

STRESSFUL SITUATIONS

Stress is a part of life. You're never going to get rid of it, so you need to decide how you are going to handle the particular things that stress you out. Different boys react to stress in different ways, just like different boys get stressed out by different things. For example, it may not bother you that the date of the school carnival was moved back by one week, but your best friend might see this as a major stress-out situation and start freaking out.

There is a funny saying that you might see on people's Facebook wall or even on t-shirts: Keep Calm and Carry On. It's actually a great way to think about stress. First of all, don't panic. Take the time to adjust to the new situation, to see the good, the bad, and the different, and then make choices based on what seems best for you. If the problem seems too big to handle yourself, don't handle it yourself. That's what adults are for. Get them involved and you're likely to cut your stress level significantly.

All Different Bodies, All Different Brains

Every boy's brain and body are different from every other boy's brain and body. That's a fact. In fact, that's what makes you, you! And just like every boy is different, every boy has his very own strengths and weaknesses, or things he does well and things he struggles with. Some of these things are in the academic field. Some boys might be great writers, able to complete 10-page papers with no problem, while others find a two-sentence assignment a huge challenge. Some differences are in sports, where there are some boys who are just better athletes without even having to try very hard.

Some differences are just part of how a boy's body functions. For example, some boys with ADHD (Attention Deficit Hyperactivity Disorder) might have trouble sitting still and concentrating. In order to function well in school, these boys might need to take prescription medication to focus and finish their work. If you're one of those boys, it's important to remember there's not something wrong with your brain, your brain just works a little differently.

Sometimes boys have brains that make it hard for them to understand what people mean when they say things, or to understand how friendships and conversations work. Sometimes boys who have brains that work in that specific way are said to be on the Autism Spectrum. They might take medication or they might need to be told things in a certain way, or they might need to be in a classroom that is run in a way that helps their brain work best.

These differences in how different boys' brains and bodies work don't have to be stressful. When the differences do cause stress it's usually because people in the bigger world haven't spent any time thinking about how they can make sure their part of the world is accessible to people whose brains and bodies might work differently.

For example, a boy might have a body that works a little differently than other kids in his class: instead of walking, he might use a wheelchair to get around. If he lives in a house that is all on one floor with a ramp to the front door, he might not really be stressed about using a wheelchair until he shows up for the first day of high school and discovers that there is a huge flight of stairs just to get into the school! Clearly it's not the wheelchair stressing the boy out, it's the lack of thinking by the people at his school that's causing the stress.

If you've been stressed out by the difference between the way your brain or body works and the way the rest of the world works, remember that everyone has his or her own challenges. No one's brain or body is perfect no matter how it might appear to an outsider. Every single person on earth struggles with something, and while it's true that you'll probably have to keep trying twice as hard and find your own way around your personal obstacles, they have to do the same thing with their personal challenges.

What should you do if a boy who has a brain or body that might not work exactly like yours has a class with you or rides the bus with you or is in a community group with you? You might feel a little uncertain about how to treat that kid. But there isn't any one way to talk to him because each boy is an individual and each situation is different. Just think about how you'd want to be treated, and follow their lead. If you think the boy might want some help with something, ask if you can help, and make sure you listen closely to his answer. Don't assume what any boy can or can't do!

You probably know this already, but ignoring or teasing kids who are different than you won't make either you or them feel better. Every person has feelings. Every boy wants to have friends and be liked. You might find that if you go a little bit out of your way to befriend a kid whose brain or body works "different", that it's you who will gain the most from the friendship.

Moving

Moving can be a very stressful time in a boy's life. When your parents first tell you that you are going to move, you might be mad. The idea might take some getting used to. After a while, you might want to take some steps that will help you think about how the move might be good for you and for your family. Here are a few first steps:

● Look up your new town online. What is near your house? Is there anything fun there that you couldn't do in your current neighborhood? Try a cool mapping program like Google Maps which may let you get a 360 degree view of your new street, neighborhood, and town.

● Look up your new school online. See if you can memorize the names of the teachers and their pictures. You can be the new kid who knows all the teachers' names the first time you see them!

● Plan how you want to decorate your new room, maybe using some of the more grown up styles you've been thinking about.

● If you're going to move in the summer, ask if you can join a community sports league or go to activities at the local community center or library to meet some kids. That way, you don't have to wait until school starts to make friends.

As with most things in life, you'll likely discover that there are both good and bad things about moving. The bad things you've probably already thought about yourself, so here are some good things to keep in mind on this new adventure:

● This is an opportunity to reinvent yourself. No one at your new school knows anything about you. No one knows that you blew the big game or tripped in the hallway. You can build yourself a brand new reputation as the person you want to be.

● You get to make new friends. Choose carefully and you'll probably find friends who will help you navigate all the hard parts of growing up.

● Here's a chance to get closer to your parents and siblings. Since they will be the only ones you know at first, use the time to hang out with them. Play games, explore your neighborhood, and build up the bonds with the people who love you most.

Divorce

Although it isn't always as dramatic as it seems on TV, divorce can also be very hard on kids. The most important thing to remember if your parents are getting divorced is: it is never, ever, ever (are you listening?) the kids' fault. Divorce is a choice adults make for adult reasons. Even if you were super extra good and never teased your little sister again, or if you were super

BOYS SAY:

I HAD TO MOVE IN EIGHTH GRADE AND IT WASN'T SO BAD. I WAS NERVOUS AT FIRST, BUT I JUST LOOKED FOR CLUBS TO JOIN AND I MADE TWO REALLY GOOD FRIENDS JUST FOR SHOWING UP TO PLAY SOME CHESS.

-Jason, age 16

The Expert Says

Divorce is one of the most stressful things a kid can deal with, but there are ways to make the situation as easy as it can be. Here are a few tips:

● Divorce is more difficult for a family if the parents can't get along at all. Ask your parents to do their best to keep the peace when you are around.

● Be fair to both of your parents. Try not to take sides. If your parents have a disagreement, try to stay out of it.

● Accept that some changes will happen. You may have to change schools or even move. You'll get used to your life sooner if you try to look at the positive aspects of it.

● Some families have money problems as parents try to adjust to having two homes and two lives instead of one. You may have to change your spending habits and your expectations of gifts at special occassions.

● Talk to someone. Don't keep your feelings inside. There are people out there who care about you and want to help.

extra bad and made her life completely miserable, you couldn't cause (or prevent) your parents' divorce.

When parents break up, there is often a lot of shuffling around of kids, and you may have to adjust to having two homes instead of one, or even (later) having a new step-parent or step-siblings. This can be really difficult, especially at first. If you are having trouble with this, it's important to talk with your parents directly, rather than acting out your feelings with bad behavior. With bad behavior you might get the attention you need, but it will be negative, not positive attention.

Drugs, Alcohol, And Other Unhealthy Stuff

Hopefully, you are looking at this and thinking, "Why are they talking about this? I am way too young to even think about stuff like that." Unfortunately that's not true for all boys. In fact, 6 percent of all kids your age say they drink alcohol on a regular basis.

Even if you don't see many people in your life smoking, drinking alcohol, or using illegal drugs, you are still exposed to advertising for alcohol and tobacco products. And you have probably seen

Using marijuana can cause memory loss and learning problems. It can also affect your coordination.

OTHER THINGS YOU SHOULD KNOW
ABOUT SMOKING, DRUGS, AND ALCOHOL:

Illegal drugs are against the law for everyone. You can be arrested for having just a little in your pocket or in your backpack, you don't even have to be using it. But for kids, cigarettes and alcohol are also against the law. In the United States, it's illegal for kids under 18 to buy cigarettes and for anyone under 21 to buy alcohol.

Advertising for both alcohol and cigarettes makes these substances look fun and grown-up. But they don't show the after effects of smoking and drinking. For example, the commercial that shows people drinking with their friends, might not show one of the friends getting arrested for driving drunk. And the billboard that shows the big, manly cowboy smoking doesn't show him a few years later dying of lung cancer.

Even if you can't think about the bad things that could happen to you in the future if you use drugs or alcohol, here are some things that could happen right away:

● Some drugs can hurt your brain and heart.

● Smoking is expensive and makes your breath, hair, and clothes stink.

● Alcohol and drugs may help you forget your problems for a little while, but they make it harder to think things through and make good decisions.

● Some boys find it hard to stop taking drugs or smoking even if they want to. Then it becomes an addiction and makes it more difficult for them to become the strong, healthy men they want to be.

movies and TV shows that show people using illegal drugs. So you probably know some things about alcohol and drugs, even if they haven't touched your life directly.

The best place to get information about smoking, drugs, and alcohol is from an adult you trust. They especially need to know if someone asks you to try these things. It's important—but not always easy—to say "no" to drugs.

It's especially hard if there are lots of drugs around you. If this is true for you, talk with the adults that are responsible for taking care of you about changing things in your environment (like where you live, where you go to school and what adults you are around) to help you stay drug-free. Even if you can't move or change schools, they can help you think up ways to make your environment safer; for example changing how you walk to school or finding different activities to be involved in after school.

One of the ways boys are pressured to use drugs is by someone presenting drinking, smoking or getting high as an adult thing to do. But facing your problems head on, and being "in the moment" (instead of being tuned out by illegal substances) is the best way to show how grown up you are.

The Expert Says

Lots of boys at this age like to try things that adults consider to be "risky" behavior. If you are looking to gain more independence, keep in mind that there are safe, constructive ways to do it. Don't feel like drugs or alcohol are the best way to "test your limits."

Super-Stressed Families

Every family has stress, but some families have much more stress to deal with than others. For example, some families have to cope with having very little money, someone in the family drinking too much or using drugs, homelessness, or living in a neighborhood with a lot of crime. Sometimes (not always) situations like this make it hard for the adults in the family to be consistent with discipline and providing for kids' needs, even if they are trying very hard. Sometimes these adults need help so that they can be the kind of parents they want to be.

If you are afraid of someone in your family, or aren't getting your basic needs (clothing, food, going to the doctor) met, or your family is super-stressed in some way, it's very important that you talk to someone. Your school guidance counselor or school nurse can be good people to start with. It might be really hard to ask for help, but it is very brave. Kids from stressed out families do NOT have to be messed up.

Handling Stressful Situations

Hopefully not too many boys reading this book will find themselves in the super-stressed family situations we just talked about. Even so, most boys have some things in their lives that make them feel anxious and stressed out.

If you find yourself having trouble managing the feelings of worry about things in your life, you might want to ask your parents to help you come up with coping strategies to help you deal with stress. Sometimes even using very simple tools can help you feel a lot better.

For example, sometimes it can be helpful to keep a stress log, which is basically a mini calendar where you write down what's bothering you when you feel especially worried. This can help you find patterns of what causes you to worry. Here's an example, if you're always stressed out on Thursday nights and you didn't know why, keeping a stress log might help you realize it's because

BOYS SAY:

TAKING TESTS STRESSES ME OUT SO THE NIGHT BEFORE A BIG TEST I TRY TO GET ALL MY OTHER WORK DONE QUICKLY SO I CAN TOTALLY CONCENTRATE ON MY STUDYING. I ALSO TRY TO REMEMBER THAT IT'S MY OVERALL QUALITY OF WORK THAT WILL MAKE MY GRADE, NOT JUST ONE TEST.

-Tony, age 14

you have pop quizzes on Friday in math, your hardest subject. If you know that, you can use that information to figure out a way to lessen your stress trigger. In this case, you might decide to get extra help in math so it doesn't seem so hard and make you so stressed out. You could also approach this situation in another way: you could do all the rest of your homework for the week before Thursday night so that you would be a little calmer on Friday since you have less to do. The key is to figure out what is causing your personal worries and try to make them a little easier on yourself.

Stress And Your Friends

Part of being a good friend is helping your friends through their stressful times. One great way to do this is by just being a good listener. Most of the time your friend won't need you to give them advice and won't need you to come up with a solution. They probably just need you to really sit still and listen to what they have to say.

You can also help your friends deal with their personal stress by offering to assist them with tasks that might be overwhelming for them. You might have to help them figure out what you could do that would be helpful. For example, if your friend breaks his arm and has to spend a few days in the hospital, you could offer something like, "I could help you by going and picking up your homework at school or I could bring you some magazines to read. Does one of those sound like something that would make this day better?"

Just as your friends should expect you to be there for them during stressful times, you should expect the same things from your friends. If you need help, call them. If they need help, be there. Together you will make it through all the challenging times that growing up can dish out.

"I Am Driving Even Myself Crazy!" Dealing With Out Of Control Feelings

Earlier in this book we talked about the extra hormones in your body and how they might make you feel moody. You may feel cranky and ready to run away from home one minute, and want to hug everyone and do a little happy dance the next. No matter how much your teachers, your parents, and even this book reminds you "this is normal," it's still no fun.

There are things you can do with this extra emotional energy though. Some things that many boys find works for them:

● Try not to get too overtired or too hungry. Hunger and tiredness can cause crankiness all by themselves, and adding them to your hormonal mix makes things much worse! If you feel like you are starting to lose control of your emotions, get yourself a healthy (read: non-sugary) snack and a big glass of water. Sometimes just sitting down for a minute to eat and drink is enough to let your emotions settle back to normal.

● Remember that feelings are not good or bad, they just are. Yes, it's more fun to feel happy than to feel sad. But it isn't wrong to feel sad. In fact, feelings give you information about yourself and your world. For example, if you always feel irritated or angry after you spend time with a certain friend, maybe there is something happening that you need to talk with that friend about.

● Writing in a journal can help you deal with strong emotions. Writing about what is going on with your feelings not only can help release some of the extra emotional energy but also can help you figure things out. If you are worried about someone reading what you've written, find a good hiding spot for your journal and get one with a lock on it. It may not be the best idea to take it to school with you because if you lose your backpack, you could lose your privacy along with it.

IS IT OKAY TO CRY?

This is a question a lot of boys ask because this is the age when people start telling them, "you're getting to be a man now, you have to stop all the tears."
You don't have to stop all the tears. In fact, it's really important to cry when you need to. Crying is a release of strong feelings, and if you don't ever have that release, it can cause you problems in your mental and physical health.

It's unfortunate that there are some people who will make you feel worse if you cry in front of them, or make it harder for you by teasing you. If you are around a lot of people like that, it can help to make a deal with a really good friend. Agree that part of your friendship is being each other's "safespace" and that you will never tease each other about crying.

KNOW THE FACTS

The tears you cry because you are sad have different chemicals in them than tears that form when your eyes water. Crying actually releases chemicals that your body is trying to get rid of. So think of crying as "taking out the trash" so your body feels better. Don't keep the trash around. Cry if you need to.

● Sometimes physical activity helps get out all your stored up emotional energy when nothing else can. That might even be why schools started having recess! You can shoot hoops, or ride your bike, or even just go for a long walk. If you're at home and can't get away and do anything else, sometimes just yelling into a pillow will work wonders!

● Talking can help, too. If you just want to let off steam, your best friend might be able to help you. If you need some guidance or advice, a trusted adult who respects your boundaries is also a good choice. If you are having particularly strong feelings, a trained professional, such as your school counselor or a psychologist should be able to help you sort out your feelings and give you some suggestions for making your emotional life easier.

● If nothing else works, get involved in a fun activity that will get your mind off of your strong feelings. You can play a musical instrument, listen to your favorite CD, read, or complete an art project. Overall, try not to dwell on your feelings. Chances are in an hour you'll feel differently.

"Try not to become a man of success but a man of value."
— ALBERT EINSTEIN

KNOW THE FACTS

Emotional outbursts are normal as you learn to cope with all the changes happening in your life, but you can also learn to express those emotions more appropriately by identifying the triggers that cause you to react aggressively.

Conclusion

You are just getting to know yourself in these years and you are going to find out you have many amazing qualities. You are different than anyone else on the planet and it's this uniqueness (and not your big muscles or acting tough) that puts you on the road to being a real man.

Some men like to watch sports and some men like to play sports. Some men hate sports and would rather spend their time on woodworking projects or playing the guitar. Some men think flowers are stinky and some men love to spend time arranging them. Some men love hunting and some men are vegetarians. None of these men are wrong.

Respect the way you are inside and say good things to yourself. Try to find and be around people who appreciate you and what you have to give. You are growing now and you have more growing to do, but you are on your way to becoming a man, a strong and caring force in the world.

RESOURCES AND FURTHER READING

Books

Feed Your Head: Some Excellent Stuff on Being Yourself
By Earl Hipp
(Hazelden, 1991)
This is an older book, but it has a ton of helpful information about resisting peer pressure.

Our Boys Speak
by John Nikkah
(St Martins, 2000)
This book is made up of letters and essays written by young boys. It is broken up into sections by topics like siblings, peer pressure, depression, and school violence. You might find it interesting how many other boys are having feelings and struggles just like yours!

Websites

Name of Website: Preteen Health Talk

Where is it? http://www.pamf.org/preteen/

Who runs it? The Palo Alto Medical Foundation

Lots of information about your changing body can be found here. Also includes sections on your feelings, growing up, and sharing. Another unique feature of this site is that it includes books and movies reviewed by both kids and parents! Also includes a special educational resource for parents and teachers about bullying prevention.

Name of Website: Are you a working teen?

Where is it? http://www.cdc.gov/niosh/docs/97-132/

Who runs it? National Institute for Occupational Safety and Health

Useful information about health and safety in the workplace; a perfect introduction as you prepare for your first job.

Name of Website: BAM! Body And Mind

Where is it? http://www.cdc.gov/bam/

Who runs it? Department of Health and Human Services

This is a huge site that includes information about diseases, food and nutrition, stress, family matters, and conflict resolution (getting along). Also includes games and quizzes and really fun interactive stuff like a create your own activity calendar, an interactive game that tests your bully smarts, and a stress-o-meter quiz.

Name of website: Guys Read

Where is it? http://www.guysread.com/

What is it? A web-based literacy program for boys founded by author and First National Ambassador of Young People's Literature Jon Scieszka. Their mission is to help boys become self-motivated, lifelong readers.

Name of website: What Do You Like?

Where is it? http://www.bls.gov/k12/

Who runs it? Bureau of Labor Statistics

You can find career information about many different types of jobs here, written especially for kids.

Name of website: Environmental Kids

Where is it? http://www.epa.gov/students/index.html

Who runs it? The Environmental Protection Agency

This site is about things you can do to make your environment safer for you and your family. It includes information on recycling, water use, and solid waste. Includes helpful fact-based information (like for school reports) as well as explanations of projects you can get involved in yourself.

Meet the Author and Illustrator

Kelli Dunham is a nurse, stand-up comic, and author of two books, *How to Survive and Maybe Even Love Nursing School* and *How to Survive and Maybe Even Love Your Life as a Nurse.* She has worked as a primary care and home visiting nurse with first-time new moms. She has lived in Port-au-Prince, Haiti, Ohio, Oklahoma, Florida, Portland, Oregon, New York, and on a houseboat in Philadelphia. In her spare time she likes to read and skateboard, and she would really, really like to learn to play the banjo.

Steve Bjorkman has illustrated more than 70 books for children, including picture books such as *Good Night, Little One*, easy readers such as *Thanksgiving Is…*, and series such as Mama Rex and T. Steve is also well known for illustrating greeting cards. More than 100 million of his greeting cards for Recycled Paper Greetings have been sold.

Index

About Applesauce Press

Good ideas ripen with time. From seed to harvest, Applesauce Press creates books with beautiful designs, creative formats, and kid-friendly information. Like our parent company, Cider Mill Press Book Publishers, our press bears fruit twice a year, publishing a new crop of titles each spring and fall.

"Where Good Books Are Ready for Press"

Visit us on the web at
www.cidermillpress.com
or write to us at
12 Spring Street, PO Box 454
Kennebunkport, Maine 04046